ANIMAL SIGNALS

Jeremy Cherfas

CASSELL

Contents

Note to the Reader

In this book there are some words in the text which are printed in **bold** type. This shows that the word is listed in the Glossary on page 31. The glossary gives a brief explanation of important words which may be new to you.

Cassell Publishers Limited
Villiers House, 41/47 Strand,
London WC2N 5JE, England

Text © Jollands Editions 1991
Illustrations © Cassell Publishers Limited 1991

First published 1991

British Library Cataloguing in Publication Data
Cherfas, Jeremy
    Animal signals. – (How animals behave)
    1. Animals. Communication. Behavioural aspects
    I. Title   II. Series
    591.59

ISBN 0–304–31877–9

Editorial planning by Jollands Editions
Designed by Alison Anholt-White

Typeset by Fakenham Photosetting Ltd
Colour origination by Golden Cup Printing Co., Ltd,
  Hong Kong
Printed in Great Britain by Eagle Colourbooks Ltd.
  Glasgow

Front Cover: An Australian koala with its young. The baby clings to its mother's back until the end of its first year. Communication is by touch.
(Photo by G. Pizzey, Bruce Coleman Ltd.)

Back Cover: The author (Photo by Rachel Pearcey)

Introduction

What do we mean by communication? It is a very hard word to define. Usually, communication is about news, it tells you what is going on. The same is true for animals. Communication tells them what is going on.

Communication needs signals, and different sorts of signal do different jobs. Because light travels in straight lines, visual signals work only if the sender and the receiver can see one another. Sound can travel round corners and through things, so it can carry a message even if the sender is hidden. Perhaps that is why birds in the trees sing so much. Smells can last a long time, so they are good for a long-term message. Touch only works for animals that are already close together. Each kind of signal has advantages and disadvantages, and there are many different kinds.

There is the smell a dog leaves on every lamp-post, and the sight of a peacock's tail. Spiders send **vibration** messages by plucking the strings of their webs. Even the bitter taste of a poisonous fruit carries a message. This book will show you some of the ways in which animals communicate, and some of the things they communicate about.

The long, banded tail of the ring-tailed lemur of Madagascar acts as a visual signal to other lemurs. The tail is held upright like a flag, so lemurs in a group can all see each other.

The peacock is the male of the common peafowl. He displays his tail feathers as a visual signal to entice females to mate with him.

1 | Messages and Meanings

Why do creatures communicate? Often, it helps them to decide what to do next. If one bird sees another across the garden one spring day they have choices to make. If both are male, they may fight. If one is male and the other female, they may court.

The male who lives there sings his song, which tells other males to keep away. But the same song attracts females who are looking for a mate. The song is a signal that has a message: 'I am a male bird and I live here'. But the message has different meanings depending on who hears it. To another male, it means 'there is a rival'. To a female, it means 'there is a mate'. Either way, because of the communication the listening bird knows more about the world. It has received information.

That is a good example of communication, but things are not always so simple. Fruit often changes colour when it is ripe. A bird will leave strawberries alone when they are green, but eat them when they are red. So would you. But is the strawberry sending a message?

The male eastern meadowlark of North America likes to sing from a high perch, where he can be seen displaying his bright colouring.

North Atlantic gannets live packed close together in colonies. Their large beaks are ideal for catching fish. They also use them to threaten other gannets if they get too close.

I think so, because the red colour indicates that the fruit is ripe. The strawberry gives the animal food, and the animal spreads the strawberry seeds. But the seeds must be ready and able to survive before the animal eats them, so when the seeds are ready the strawberry changes colour.

Different kinds of signal

Sometimes, an animal's message is meant to be received loud and clear. There is no mistaking the roar of a lion. Other times, it may want to keep the signal secret. A mother hen clucking to her chicks does so quietly, so she will not attract foxes or cats. The lion and the hen both use sound to communicate, but signals come in many varieties.

This book is about the variety of animal communications and signals, but it is not about human language. Words are what we use most often to communicate, and language is a marvellous way of passing information from one person to another. Other animals don't have anything as complicated as human language, but they have different talents, as you will discover.

The brilliantly-coloured quetzal of Central America feeds on small fruit which it picks while on the wing. To the bird, red means ripe and ready to be eaten.

A male spring peeper treefrog of North America, at the start of the breeding season. This is the time when the males sing in chorus to attract females. The sound is amplified by the enlarged throat sac.

Many animals and plants use visual signals, but some of them are invisible to us. Flowers that look plain white or blue to us look quite different to a honeybee. The bee can see stripes and patterns on the petals that we cannot. The stripes guide the bee to the nectar, and in exchange for food the bee **pollinates** the flower.

Worker honeybees are attracted to certain flowers by their markings. Their main job is to collect pollen in a pocket or pollen basket and take it back to the hive. At the same time they pollinate the flowers they visit.

A male European robin attacking a stuffed bird. Even though it is not a live bird, the robin sees it as another male intruder, because of the red feathers. The North American robin is larger than the European species. It has a grey back and a brick-red breast.

Simple signals

Sometimes a visual signal is far simpler than it seems at first. A male robin will violently attack any other robin who strays into his **territory**. What is it about the other robin that makes him so angry? The red breast is all that matters. If you put out a stuffed robin whose breast feathers have been dyed brown, the resident will ignore it. But if you simply attach a clump of red feathers to a branch, with no bird behind them, the robin will attack the feathers as if they were a rival robin.

Biologists have discovered many instances where an animal pays attention to only one aspect of what it sees. Sticklebacks are little fish that live in streams. In spring, the male becomes much more brightly coloured, and develops a bright red belly to show he is ready to breed. Like the robin, he will ignore another stickleback without a red belly, but he will attack a very crude model, even if it looks nothing like a fish, as long as it is red underneath.

Chain messages

A quick reply is not always the best way to respond to a message. If you are choosing a mate you want to make sure you are getting the best you can. One way to do that is to have a chain of signals, with each link providing more information.

The stickleback, who is so eager to chase off anything with a red belly, behaves very differently to a female. Her belly is silver, and often swollen with eggs. The male swims up to her, then he darts away. Usually she does not follow him at first, so he swims back to her, then away again. This is called the zig-zag dance.

The male is trying to lead the female to the nest he has built. If she is attracted by his zig-zag dance, she will follow him to the nest. Now he shows her what a fine nest it is, pointing at it and quivering. She may

Sticklebacks are small fish found in the northern hemisphere. A male stickleback sees a rival male approaching. He puts on a threatening display by raising the sharp spines on his back. This is his way of saying 'Go away! This is my territory.'

With the rival out of the way, the male stickleback dances in zig-zag fashion towards the nest he has made. He shows the entrance of his nest to a female whose silvery belly is large with eggs.

decide against his nest, and swim away. But if she stays, he points into the entrance of the nest.

She looks inside, and prefers nests with eggs in them. They mean that this male has been successful and has attracted other females to lay in his nest. If she lays there for him, maybe her sons will inherit his attractiveness and get more females when they start to breed.

Again the female has the chance to leave without laying her eggs. But if she stays she will swim through the nest, lay her eggs, and swim off. The male looks after their offspring on his own.

The communication chain of the stickleback gives the female more and more information, so she can decide whether to mate with this male or look for another. At each step in the chain, she can stay or leave. If she stays, the male sends his next signal. If she goes away, he starts looking for another female.

Greatly excited, the male stickleback urges the female to enter the nest and lay her eggs. If she finds that there are eggs already there she will lay her own eggs as she swims through the nest.

After the female has laid her eggs, she departs and the male immediately follows her. He then fertilizes the eggs the female has laid. The male will then tend the nest and look after the offspring.

Identity badges

Visual signals are often a sort of identity badge; they tell whoever sees them something about the sender. In the forests of West Africa there are more than thirty different kinds of small monkey. The different **species** are all closely related, and if you saw them from far away you would have a hard time telling them apart. Close-up, however, you can see that they each have very distinct markings, especially on the face. These markings announce the species they belong to.

Faces, especially the faces of **primates**, carry very important messages. An angry person looks different from a happy person. You communicate how you feel without using words, just with visual signals.

Left: De Brazza's monkeys from West Africa are small and slender. With its mouth closed, it is hard to tell what this monkey is feeling or thinking. There are many closely-related species of small monkeys like this one, and they all have slightly different face markings.

Right: The Diana monkeys of West Africa live in trees in large groups. The threatening expression on this animal's face is quite enough to make enemies keep their distance.

3 Sound Signals

Sound signals spread out from the animal making the noise, and can go through bushes and leaves, so sound is a very good way of broadcasting a message. Most birds use sound to proclaim their presence, but bird song can communicate much more information than that.

Wrens, for example, are tiny birds that might flitter about in the bottom of a hedge. The male wren has a long and loud song that he uses to attract females. And the females seem to prefer males with more complicated songs. The more tunes he can sing, the more she likes him. A male with a very good song might attract two or three females to mate with him and nest on his territory.

This is a bearded Belgium bantam cock. The sound signal of the cock crowing in the early hours of the morning has been known to people for centuries. The ancient Romans divided the day into a number of parts, one of which was the hour before dawn when cocks begin to crow.

A scientist recording bird-song in an English woodland. Most bird species have quite simple songs consisting of one or two notes. But some species, such as the chaffinch, the blackbird and the nightingale, have songs that are very varied and melodious.

A whale of a song

From the tiny wren to the giant humpback whale might seem like an enormous leap, but male humpback whales seem to use their songs in a very similar way to wrens. The song of a humpback is very long and complicated, and all the whales in one part of the world sing their own version of the same song. Males in another part of the ocean sing a different song. But wherever they are, the males seem to change their song slightly each year. Nobody knows how they agree on that year's song.

It seems that the whales are holding a sort of underwater song contest, and, like the wren, the one with the best song will attract the most females.

A scientist near Vancouver Island, Canada, with some of the equipment used for recording the underwater sounds made by whales and dolphins. The songs made by humpback whales may last an hour or more, and a whale repeats them over and over without making mistakes. These remarkable sounds are still a great mystery, and the scientists have not yet discovered what the sounds mean.

There are over sixty species of wrens and they are found throughout North America and Europe. The song of these tiny birds is continuous and varied. In many of the species the female wren joins the male in song.

A humpback whale making a spectacular leap out of the water, known as a breach. Humpbacks do this over and over again. Are they trying to get rid of pests attached to their skin, or are they sending a sound message with a splash? Perhaps they are just having fun, as we do when we plunge or dive into water. Humpback whales are found worldwide, but they seem to avoid the cold waters of the polar regions.

Alarm calls

As well as advertising, sound is often used as a warning, and when they are threatened many animals make special noises called alarm calls. Other animals who hear the alarm call will be on the lookout. That includes animals of completely different species. Often you can see all sorts of birds fly away after one has given an alarm call. But one animal, the vervet monkey, has a set of alarm calls so advanced it is like a very simple language.

Vervet monkeys live in East Africa, where they have four main enemies apart from people: leopards, eagles, snakes and baboons. The different enemies attack in different ways. Leopards, for example, hide and catch vervets in the grass, while eagles swoop from the sky and pluck them from the trees. So the vervet should take different action to escape the different **predators**. If there is a leopard, the monkeys will be safe in the trees, but if there is an eagle that is the most dangerous place to be.

The monkeys make a different alarm call for each predator. When one gives the leopard alarm call, the others scurry into the trees. But when they hear the eagle alarm call, they come out of the trees into the grass. They do the right thing even when the alarm call comes from a loudspeaker and there are no predators to be seen. So the alarm call is a bit like a word in a human language, and when the monkey hears a particular call it behaves as if it had seen that predator.

Vervet monkeys of East Africa are on the look out for enemies all the time. They have one kind of alarm call if eagles are spotted. Then they all go down from the trees to the ground where the eagles cannot catch them.

Vervet monkeys in the grass may be attacked by leopards. If one is seen, they make a different alarm call. Then the group will scamper off to safety in the trees.

Sounds we cannot hear

Just as bees can see colours that people cannot, many animals use sound that we cannot hear. Dolphins, in addition to the clicks and whistles and squeaks that we can hear, also make sounds that are too high-pitched for our ears. These high-pitched noises are called **ultrasounds**, and the dolphins use them to keep in touch with other members of their school.

Dolphins also use ultrasounds to find food, listening for the echoes bouncing off nearby fish. Bats do the same, and this technique of using sound to find your way about, at night or in murky water, is called **echolocation**. But although it provides information, it is not really a form of communication.

A long-eared bat in flight amongst foliage. Bats have poor vision but make up for this with their highly-developed system of echolocation. Their large ears receive continuous echoes of the high-pitched sounds sent out from their mouths. As a result, they can fly through forests without hitting the trees. Long-eared bats are found in North America and Europe.

A Queensland blossom bat feeding on banana flowers in northern Queensland, Australia. Not all bats rely on echolocation, and this species has good vision and a strong sense of smell. The ears are small compared with those of the long-eared bat shown above.

At the other end of the scale from ultrasounds are noises too low for us to hear. These are called **infrasounds**. If you get very close to a herd of African elephants, you may feel a slight rumbling in your body. It is caused by elephant infrasound, a low-pitched boom that rolls out across the **savannah**. Elephants use infrasound to send all sorts of messages between the widely scattered members of a herd. Females on heat, for example, advertise the fact with an infrasound message that brings bull elephants from five kilometres or more away.

A herd of African elephants on the move in Namibia. These animals fan out their huge ears as a signal to frighten away an approaching enemy. They also wave their ears to keep cool and to shake off flies.

4 | Chemical Signals

Chemical signals are useful because they can be carried long distances through air or water. And the source of the signal may stay behind even after the animal has moved on. So chemical signals are often used to mark the boundaries of a territory.

Marking boundaries

This may have started by accident. If an animal had a nest or den in the middle of its territory, it might be more hygienic to go far away from the nest to get rid of waste products such as faeces or urine. These wastes often smell, and might convey the message 'Territory occupied!' to a passing animal, and this would save it having to explore and perhaps fight.

Today, animals make scent marks in all sorts of ways. Some, like the hippopotamus, simply scatter their dung as far as they can. Others, like the gazelles of East Africa, make neat piles of their dung. Tom-cats and tigers spray urine as high as they can. And many animals have special **glands** for making long-lasting chemical marks. In all cases, the message is the same: 'Territory occupied!'

This East African animal is a Kirk's dik-dik. He is rubbing a gland near his eye against a grass-stalk. These small antelopes mark their territory by leaving chemical messages in this manner.

This magnificent Indian tiger is spray-marking his territory. This is a warning message to other tigers that happen to be passing.

17

Somewhere to settle

Often, the response will be to go away, but sometimes the animal is looking for an occupied territory. Barnacles are small animals related to crabs, and you might have seen them encrusting rocks at the seaside. They start their life as tiny **larvae** drifting in the water. Eventually, they must find somewhere to settle down and change into an adult, but there is a lot of water and few good places to settle.

One way of finding a home is to go where other barnacles have found one, and that is what the larva does. Adult barnacles give out a chemical into the water. When the larva picks up this chemical message, it swims down until it reaches the adults. Then it glues itself down and begins the process of becoming an adult itself. If it does not receive the signal to settle, it wanders about till it dies.

Barnacles hanging down from a floating log.

A male emperor moth (orange) with a female (grey) nearby.

Like gypsy moths, the male emperor moth is attracted to the female by a chemical known as a pheromone. The feathery antennae of the male receive the chemical signal from the female when she is ready to mate. The antennae are designed to receive signals, like television aerials. Emperor moths are found in Europe and Asia.

Finding a mate

Chemical signals are very important to animals looking for a mate. A female on heat often smells different from one who is not ready to mate, and that sends the males a message. Butterflies and moths use chemical messages to attract males to them.

When the female gypsy moth is ready to mate she sits on a branch and starts releasing a chemical called gyplure. This blows away on the breeze. The male gypsy moth has feathery **antennae** on his head, designed to sieve the air for smells. When a **molecule** of gyplure – a single molecule – lands on his antennae, the male sets off.

He flies upwind, because that is where the signal is coming from. When the signal stops, he has flown past the female. So he stops and searches visually for her. If he is the first to find her, they mate.

Using a chemical in this way saves the moths time and energy. The female sits still and lets the wind carry her message far and wide. The male does not waste his time searching when there are no females nearby. Communication by **pheromone**, as this chemical signal is called, makes their lives more efficient.

Harvester ants from East Africa. Two ants from different colonies engage in a skirmish. The ant on guard has recognized an intruder by sniffing with its antennae.

Colony smells

Chemical signals, like gyplure, are often identity badges as well as messages that there is a female around. They tell the male that it is a gypsy moth female, and he ignores the pheromones of other kinds of moth. Many species use smells in this way, especially those that live together in colonies.

A large ants' nest, for example, will have guards at all the entrances. The guards touch each ant that passes with their antennae. What they are doing is sniffing the ant, to see whether it carries the correct chemical badge. Only if it belongs to the colony will the guards let it pass.

Mammals too use odour in this way. Mongooses have a special gland near the base of the tail. This produces a smelly **secretion** which the mongoose uses to mark its territory, itself, and sometimes other members of its pack. One mongoose can tell, simply by sniffing another, what sex it is and whether it belongs to the same pack. Within a pack, the mongooses can probably tell one another apart by smell.

A male and female yellow mongoose from Namibia. They greet each other by using the sense of smell. This tells them whether they belong to the same pack, and whether they have met each other before.

People and smells

People often assume that their own sense of smell is very poor. Actually, we are very good at receiving chemical messages. Many people use perfumes to add to, or sometimes to hide, their own smells, and those perfumes often use the chemical messages of other species, the scents of flowers and the odours of animals. I sometimes wonder what kind of messages people are trying to send when they wear different perfumes. But even without perfumes, smell plays an important part in human life.

Just as members of the same ant colony smell the same, so members of a human family share their odour. A mother can correctly pick out the smell of her own child, and even a newborn baby prefers the smell of its own mother to that of another mother.

Although smell is important to humans, often in ways we find hard to understand, it is much more important to other animals. When I take my dog for a walk, and see his quivering, twitching nose exploring everything he pokes it at, I wonder what exactly all those wonderful smells tell him. What do the marks he leaves tell other dogs? I don't suppose I will ever know.

Two young prairie dogs at the entrance mound of one of their vast burrows. These North American rodents live in large groups. When two of them meet, they sniff at each other to find out if they are from the same group.

5 | Touch

Touch is another way of sending a message. When animals touch each other they can send and receive information, but sometimes touch consists of vibrations sent through whatever the animal is standing on. Many male spiders spin a special line to send love songs to a female they are interested in.

A small male spider courting a large female. He sends vibrations along the silken thread between them as a message to the female that he wants to mate with her.

Vibrations

The female spider sits at the centre of her web, feeling for the vibrations caused by an insect struggling to escape from the sticky threads. If the male simply walked on to the web, she might mistake him for a meal. So he spins a line and sticks it to her web. Then he plucks the line, sending a special set of vibrations to the female. If she is ready to mate, she may come over and investigate.

Other spiders, which don't spin webs, also use touch to communicate. A spider called *Cupiennius* uses vibration to find and court its mate. These spiders wander about the leaves of banana plants at night. The male drums a song on his leaf, which vibrates gently through the whole tree. The females can detect very slight vibrations, and one who feels the male's message drums back a signal of her own. He uses that to decide which leaf she is on, and moves off to find her. They keep in touch with their drumming duet until he reaches her and they mate.

Soothing touches

Touch plays a very different part in the life of the hamadryas baboon. These animals live on the rocky cliffs of Ethiopia. The big males try to keep a group of females for themselves, and touch is one of the signals they use to do so.

Each day, the male will sit and groom each of his females, carefully picking through her fur in search of parasites and dirt, which he removes. The more females he has, the more time he has to spend fighting off rival males, which leaves less time for grooming his females. But the females expect a certain amount of grooming each day. If they don't get it, they will wander off to a younger male who has more time to touch and groom them.

While he is able to sit and groom the female, the male is communicating his strength and ability to keep other males away. If he has no time to groom, it is probably because he is losing his grip on his females.

Giraffes 'neck' as part of their courtship ritual.
Photographed in Kenya.

The male hamadryas baboon uses the sense of touch to keep his females contented. He spends a lot of time grooming them, keeping their fur clean and free of parasites. Hamadryas baboons are found in Somalia.

The dance of the bees

Honeybees have a special problem, and a remarkable communication system to solve it. The problem is to find food and use it efficiently. New patches of flower come into bloom through the summer, and the bees have to find them and then collect the pollen and nectar. In the morning, worker bees called scouts fly out from the hive and scour the countryside. When one finds a patch of flowers in bloom, she comes back to the hive to recruit many workers to gather the food. A drop of the food she has gathered tells them what the flowers smell like, but how does she tell the new recruits where to go?

Karl von Frisch, an Austrian scientist, watched honeybees very carefully, and discovered that scouts do a special dance when they return from a successful search. The scout runs along the honeycomb, waggling her **abdomen** from side to side.

Honeybees fly to find food and cannot lay trails for other bees to follow. When a worker has found a good source of food, she returns to the hive and performs a dance which tells the other bees where the food is.

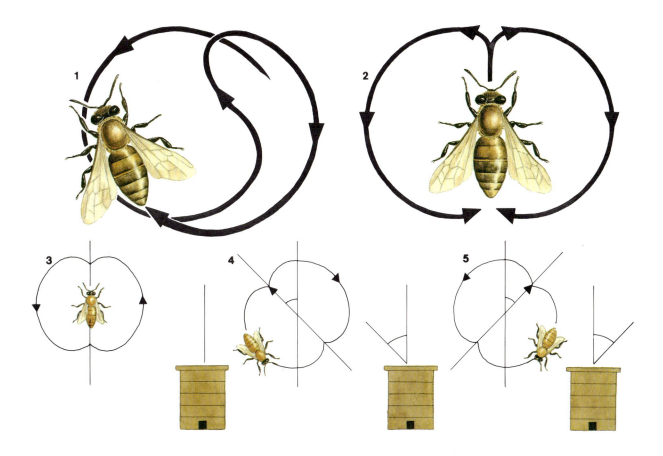

Then she circles round and runs along in the same direction again. She does this over and over, with the workers following what von Frisch called the waggle dance.

Von Frisch discovered that the direction of the waggling run told the workers the direction of the food, and the number of waggles told them how far away from the hive it was. It seems that the workers pick up the information by touching the body of the scout as she dances in the darkness inside the hive. People can decode the information by watching and counting, but the bees do it by touch and smell.

Von Frisch called the bees' communication a dance language, and although it cannot communicate many things it certainly helps the bees to make good use of their food supply. Scouts use the same dance language to tell the bees when they have found a new place for the hive.

1. When the food source is close to the hive, the scout performs a round dance.
2. When the food is far away, she dances in the form of a figure eight. The speed of the dance indicates the distance of the food. 3, 4, 5. The scout points in a definite direction from the hive, while waggling her abdomen. The angle is related to the position of the sun. The other bees navigate by using the sun as a marker.

6 | False Signals

Not all signals are genuine. An insect that looks like a leaf is sending a false signal. A hungry bird would eat the insect, but will ignore a leaf. The insect is communicating the fact that it is inedible, even though it actually is good to eat. Many animals and plants pretend to be things that they are not.

Some hungry birds like to eat insects. But this leaf insect stays alive by looking exactly like a leaf. It comes from Malaysia.

A British cuckoo often lays her one egg in the nest of a reed warbler. Her egg is slightly larger than the others, but the markings are very similar.

A young cuckoo being fed by its reed warbler foster-parent. The poor reed warbler has been deceived by the wily cuckoo, and has done all the cuckoo's work.

The wily cuckoo

Cuckoos are experts at sending misleading messages. The cuckoo lays her eggs in the nest of another bird. When the egg hatches, the cuckoo chick kills the other nestlings, but the foster parents continue to look after the monstrous cuckoo chick.

Why don't the parents get rid of the cuckoo egg? Different birds have different patterns on their eggs, but the cuckoo's egg matches the eggs of the foster parents she has chosen. Some cuckoos almost always put their eggs in the nests of reed warblers, and their eggs look like reed warblers' eggs. Others lay in meadow pipits' nests, and their eggs look like the eggs of a meadow pipit. The hosts cannot tell that they have a cuckoo in the nest.

When the cuckoo egg hatches, it soon grows into a chick far bigger than its foster parents. Why don't they abandon it now? Perhaps because they cannot. Parent birds respond to the brightly coloured markings inside the throat of a young nestling. The cuckoo has the same markings, often even brighter, and that is all the parent birds pay attention to. This is an example of a simple message that has gone wrong for the foster parent but not for the cuckoo.

Mimics and wreckers

There are many other examples of animals sending false messages. Two that you might not know about are slave-making ants and firefly wreckers.

Slave-making ants raid other ants' nests to steal their young. The slave-makers take the young back to work for them in their own nest. But ants' nests, you will remember, have guards that will not let strange ants in. To get past them and into the heart of the nest where the young are, the slave-makers spray a chemical that smells like the guards' own identity smell.

Fireflies use a flashing light signal to attract a mate. But some flashing lights are not mates. They are hungry females who **mimic** the flashing pattern of a different species to entice males of that species to their death. Years ago, on stormy coasts, people called wreckers would put out false lights to lure sailing ships on to the rocks. Then the wreckers would come and take the cargo. False information can be very dangerous.

A female firefly giving off her strong light signal. The male firefly also gives off light but it is much weaker.

Although it is harmless and has no sting, the wasp beetle mimics the wasp in its appearance. Its wasplike colouring is a kind of bluff that acts well as a means of self-defence. These insects are to be found in the woodlands of Europe and North America.

7 | Communicating with Animals

Have you heard of King Solomon's ring? It was a magic ring that allowed whoever wore it to talk to, and understand, all the animals in the world. People who study animal behaviour closely are learning to understand animal communications. And of course it is possible to teach animals to understand our language. But it is easy to make mistakes.

Happy or scared?

When the first chimpanzee went up into space, the newspapers showed a photograph of it grinning from ear to ear with all its teeth showing. Everybody thought it was very happy. But scientists who had looked at chimpanzees for a long time had a different explanation.

In the wild, the only time they saw a chimpanzee grin like that was when it was terrified. The grin is a signal. It means, 'I am very frightened, please leave me alone.' And usually the chimp that is frightening the grinning chimp will do just that and go. A happy chimp has a completely different kind of grin, and keeps its teeth covered. So you have to be careful when you think you know what an animal means.

There is no mistaking the look of pleasure on the faces of these Siamang gibbons from South East Asia.

Chimpanzees are very intelligent and can learn from their human relations. The chimp plays this game happily as there is a reward of a grape for skilful aiming.

Clever Hans

A different problem crops up when an animal understands you much better than you think. In the 1890s, a man called Wilhèlm von Osten had a calculating horse. Von Osten wrote sums on a blackboard, and the horse tapped its hoof to give the correct answer. Von Osten honestly thought that the horse could read and do arithmetic, and he called the horse Clever Hans. Actually, von Osten was communicating the answer to Clever Hans. While the horse was tapping, von Osten leaned forward slightly, to get a better view of Hans' hoof, and when Hans was about to reach the correct answer, von Osten straightened up. Clever Hans learned the signal. He stopped tapping, and von Osten would give him a sugar lump for being so clever.

I think Clever Hans was even cleverer than von Osten thought, for understanding signals that his teacher didn't even know he was sending. Next time you see a cat or dog do something clever, think about the hidden signals that might be helping it.

In this old engraving, Morocco, the wonder horse of 1595, is stamping out the numbers shown on a pair of rolled dice.

Although we do not yet understand the 'language' that dolphins use to communicate with each other, we are learning to communicate with them. These dolphins have been trained to have fun by leaping over a pole together.

30

Astounding Facts

- Young birds in their eggs cheep to one another so that they can all hatch together.

- Whales might be able to hear the songs of other whales up to 1,000 kilometres away.

- The area covered by a bee when searching for food is, in human terms, about 130,000 square kilometres.

- Some species of mole rats bang their heads on the roofs of their tunnels to send messages to other mole rats.

- Bees normally use their waggle dance to tell other bees about nectar and pollen. But they can also use the dance to tell them where there is water, which bees need to keep the hive cool in hot weather, or where there is plant sap that can be used to repair the hive.

Glossary

abdomen: the hind part of an insect's body. In mammals, the abdomen is the belly.

antenna: one of a pair of feelers projecting from the head of insects and some water animals.

echolocation: locating objects and working out their direction and distance by means of echoes.

gland: a part of the body that makes substances used elsewhere. Wax and silk are used outside the body. Saliva usually stays inside the body to help digest food.

infrasound: a sound so low-pitched that it cannot be heard by the human ear.

larva: a young animal that looks different from its parent.

mimic: to imitate another species.

molecule: the smallest part of a substance that can exist on its own. Single molecules consist of two or more atoms joined together.

pheromone: a chemical given out by an animal, that is used to send a message.

pollinate: to transfer the pollen grains from the male parts to the female parts of a flowering plant.

predator: any animal that hunts and eats other animals. Lions are predators.

primate: a group of mammals that includes apes, monkeys and humans.

savannah: a grassy plain with few trees in a warm part of the world.

secretion: a substance, such as saliva, produced by a gland in animals or plants.

species: a class of animals or plants that look alike. Members of one species cannot usually breed with those of another species.

territory: an area of land in which an animal or group of animals live. Animals mark out and protect their territories.

ultrasound: a sound so high-pitched that it cannot be heard by the human ear.

vibration: moving continuously to and fro, or up and down.

Index

You can use this index for looking up different animals, and the parts of the world where some of them are found. Where a page number is printed in *italic* (slanting) type, it means that there is a picture of that animal on that page, as well as text.

Further Reading and Study

If you have enjoyed reading this book and want to learn more about animals and how they behave, there are several things you can do:

- You can read the other five titles in this series. They are listed on the back cover. This will widen your knowledge of animal behaviour.

- Learn all you can about the animals that interest you most. Look them up in a natural history encyclopedia or other reference book.

- Learn about other series of books dealing with wildlife, for example:
  Discovering Nature series published by Wayland
  Eyewitness Guides published by Dorling Kindersley, and by Collins in Australia
  Mysteries and Marvels of Nature published by Usborne
  Today's World published by Watts/Gloucester

- If you have a pet, increase your knowledge of animal behaviour by watching how your pet behaves.

Picture Acknowledgements

The publishers wish to thank the following photographers and agencies whose photographs appear in this book. The photographs are credited below by page number and position

Heather Angel/Biofotos: 23T. Alison Anholt-White: 30B. Ardea London Ltd: Liz and Tony Bomford 3T, 11B, John Daniels 4B, 14T, Hans and Judy Best 15B, Kenneth Fink 23B. Bruce Coleman Ltd: M. P. L. Fogden 5T, H. J. Flugel 6T, E. Breeze-Jones 7, Jane Burton 8 (both), 20T, Kim Taylor 9 (both), Rod Williams 10 TL, Mark Boulton 11T, Jeff Foott 12, 21, R. Wilmshurst 13T, Frank Greenaway 15T, Jen and Des Bartlett 16, 20B, G. Ziesler 17B, Peter Ward 19, John Markham 22, 27T, Gerald Cubitt 26. Frank Lane Picture Agency Ltd: R. Austing 4T, Frank Lane 5B, 29B, Terry Whittaker 10TR, S. McCutcheon 13, Peggy Heard 14B, D. P. Wilson 18T, Treat Davidson 24, Roger Tidman 27B, Mark Newman 29T. Nature Photographers Ltd: Roger Tidman 3B, Hugo van Lawick 17T, Paul Sterry 18B, 28T, N. A. Callow 28B.